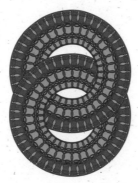

APPARITION HILL

APPARITION
HILL

MARY RUEFLE

CavanKerry ❖ Press Ltd.

Library of Congress Cataloging-in-Publication Data

Ruefle, Mary, 1952-
    Apparition Hill / Mary Ruefle.
    p. cm.
    ISBN 0-9678856-6-3
    I. Title.
PS3568.U36 A84 2001
811'.54--dc21   2001028874

Grateful acknowledgment is made to the editors of the following magazines where some of these poems first appeared: *The Black Warrior Review, The Boston Review, College English, The Denver Quarterly, The Kenyon Review, Marquee, The Michigan Quarterly Review, The Southern Humanities Review*, and the anthology *Elvis in Oz: New Stories and Poems from the Hollins Creative Writing Program.*

Front cover photograph by the author
Designed by Dede Cummings Designs

FIRST EDITION

CavanKerry Press Ltd
Fort Lee, New Jersey
www.cavankerrypress.com

For Dara

CONTENTS

Imagination at wit's end spreads its sad wings
—SAMUEL BECKETT

Relax and forget it, my friend
—CHUANG TZU

APPARITION HILL

LAPLAND

The little Lap girl wanders around picking cloudberries
while the bluethroat sings one of his hundred songs.
There are tiny white flowers too: angelica,
and the wild white ranunculus.
The reindeer eat lichen and moss under the melting snow.
Some of the lichen are a thousand years old
and do not recognize the modern world.
The geography lessons are young in comparison,
though this one is older than most, since
Lapland lies on no map and the little Lap girl
must be at least eighty by the looks of the book.
It is doubtful she remembers the day
of this photograph. The pencil-stroke of a birch
can be seen in the distance. Once in a while
she must still hear the bluethroat and think
of her childhood. Out of a hundred songs
he has not forgotten the one he sang
on an afternoon when the snow left and
the wild white ranunculus took its place.
But he is the peripheral sort
and not at the center of anything.

CUL-DE-SAC

The milkman delivered the milk.
Out of desperation, I suppose.
My mother took her squirrel stole
out of its bag and I saw her initials
on the inside satin shimmering
like the future itself.
My father took his golf clubs out of their mitts
and I saw the enormous integers
each one was assigned.
In September I got new shoes
whether I needed them or not.
In April a hat of pastel straw.
We had a carport and lived on a cul-de-sac.
I know these things are fleshless and void,
as unimportant as a mouse.
Hardly full of the farmlight and yet like
the farmlight that slips in under my door
where my bookcases are weighted with books.
My brother has a van full of rifles,
a string of wives and children
along the interstate, and I do not know
if he shaves or does not. We each think
the other has flattened a life.
I read one day that Jesus had a sister.
I wish I had her tenacity.
The woodshed shudders in the wind.
The barn is stark on the hill.
My mother's name and my father's numbers

lie in a landfill that is leveled far away.
Brother, I have been unable to attain a balance
between important and unimportant things.

DO NOT AFFECT A BREEZY MANNER

—The Elements of Style
WILLIAM STRUNK, JR. & E.B. WHITE

With the implacable rigor of a raving fantasy
I decline, and the whole world declines
with me: Time, E.B., is windswept, and
this century cannot come to life again
nor those who ate and grew in it stifle
their yawn. The table is cleared.
The king's cutlet was embossed!
That little piece of pork
had the wherewithal for frivolity
and is gone.

THE PEDANT'S DISCOURSE

Ladies, life is no dream; Gentlemen,
it's a brief folly: you wouldn't know
death's flashcard if you saw it.
First the factories close, then the mills,
then all of the sooty towns
shrivel up and fall off from the navel.
And how should I know, just because my gramma
died in one? I was four hundred miles away,
shopping. I bought a pair of black breasts
with elastic straps that slip over the shoulder.
I'm always afraid I might die at any moment.
That night I heard a man in a movie say
I have no memories and presumably he meant it.
But surely it was an act. I remember my gramma's
housedress was covered with roses. And she
remembered it too. How many times she turned
to her lap and saw the machines: the deep folds
of red shirts endlessly unfolding while they dried.
Whose flashcard is that? So, ladies and gentlemen,
the truth distorts the truth and we are in it up
to our eyebrows. I stand here before you tonight,
old and wise: cured of vain dreams, debauched,
wayward and haggard. The mind's a killjoy, if
I may say so myself, and the sun's a star,
the red dwarf of which will finally consume us.

THE SANCTITY OF MUDDLE

Especially when there was no money
she would have gone mad, but she would
pull over to the side of the road and
scrawl odd words by the light of the
glovebox; a gesture as pathetic and
affected as the lowrider gunning it
through another light. One hundred years
ago, the village maid scattered petals
in her bath while the idiot at her window
watched her disrobe. What's the difference?
All days have a certain clumsiness and
bourgeois spirit to them. Someone's besotted
in the bus john, the toilet has a warm seat
and sloshes blue below. There's a fruity
disinfectant in the air. Outside, rolls of
spring reel by. What a world! said Charles
Doughty, who is being read up front,
in back of the driver who notices the girl's
gone mad, pulling over like that in heavy
traffic, and the boy trying to beat the light
must be her brother. We behave as if
there's a large fruit still uneaten.
If there's a large fruit still uneaten
it can't be so large as that, large
enough for every last living soul
to wrap and carry. The milkmaid vanished
in her bath. The drunk loved it in the john.
Charles Doughty, for once, was left
in peace when the reader fell asleep and

what the girl wrote by the light of the
glovebox was *the sanctity of muddle is to
be admired*. Only the lowrider slipped by,
but he too was eventually stopped by a cop
who drawled *here's your autobiography kid*
while writing out the ticket.

HIDDEN TRAFFIC

                    If
the small useless bass
see the flash of my skate blade,
I see the glitter of iced grit
on the semi's mud-flap in traffic
this morning: hidden in the picture
of lives backed up
for proceeding in slush
was a czar's egg,
not to mention a Brueghel
restored to its original state
in the time it took the light to change:
the figure smalled
and the panic dissolved
like some winged thing
gone black
and back down.

LILIES OF THE NILE

for KATE CLEAVER

Birdsong is an enormous and empty spring green space...
when I say empty I mean: no one has ever died there.
Citadel of clouds over the hill. The smell of mint
in damp places. Wearing dresses and high heels
we board the little boat, pick up the oars, glance back
at the newborn asleep in the grass.
There are pieces of layer cake on our laps
and the lawn is green and half a mile long
leading down to the pond, all of it mowed. We push out.
By the time we reach the bull's eye we no longer want
what we have, have left, may have had. We drift.
I put my hand in the water and leave it there,
a god for the fish. In June of the year 1250
two thousand Saracens were slaughtered:
their washed blood left a famous citadel pink,
golden in the patch of sun that sat on it.

NOW OR NEVER

The three of us drinking anisette in a bar after visiting the maskmaker
where we tried on half a dozen plaster of Paris enigmas
and slouched now in an upholstered booth with our little liqueurs
snappy and sweet and new to the throat: fed up
at eighteen, nineteen, twenty, intoxicated, animated, bored,
when your mouth began to open then closed, kept opening then
    closing,
opening and closing without crossing the verge, without stepping
    back —
you yourself did not know how it would end, but the gesture became
    you,
never again would you resemble anyone else —
one of us looked out the window and saw (already forty years ago)
the pause, and nothing has done nothing to start it up again
though the day lasted long enough to provoke laughter and later
    disappear.

NAKED LADIES

Rousseau wanted: a cottage on the Swiss shore,
a cow and a rowboat.

Stevens wanted a crate from Ceylon full of jam
and statuettes.

My neighbors are not ashamed of their poverty
but would love to be able to buy a white horse,
a stallion that would transfigure the lot.

Darwin was dying by inches from not having anyone to talk to
about worms, and the vireo outside my window wants nothing less
than a bit of cigarette-wool for her nest.

The unattainable is apparently rising on the tips of forks
the world over...

So-and-so is wearing shoes for the first time

and Emin Pasha, in the deepest acreage of the Congo,
wanted so badly to catch a red mouse! Catch one he did
shortly before he died, cut in the throat by slavers who
wanted to kill him. *At last!* runs the diary

and it is just this *at last* we powder up and call progress.

So the boys chipped in and bought Bohr a gram of radium
for his 50th birthday.

Pissarro wanted white frames for his paintings
as early as 1882, and three francs for postage, second place.

Who wants to hear once more the sound of their mother throwing
Brussels sprouts into the tin bowl?

Was it *ping* or was it *ting*?

What would you give to smell again the black sweetpeas
choking the chain-link fence?

Because somebody wants your money.

The medallions of monkfish in a champagne sauce…

The long kiss conjured up by your body in a cast…

The paradisiacal vehicle of the sweet-trolley rolling in
as cumulous meringue is piled on your tongue
and your eye eats the amber glaze of a crème brûlée…

The forgiveness of sins, a new wife, another passport,
the swimming pool, the rice bowl

full of rice, the teenage mutant ninja turtles escaping
as you turn the page…

Oh brazen sex at the barbecue party!

Desire is a principle of selection. Who wanted *feet* in the first place?

Who wanted to stand up? Who felt like walking?

HARDER AND HARDER

Will the bridge collapse
if the last gray inch of paint is applied
as the last gray painter breathes in and not out?

Enola Gay Haggard of Glidden, Iowa
forgot to take the cookies out.
They blackened on the sheet.

It is hard to exaggerate.

All morning long he's been strapped
to the girder,
watching the strip tease of October,
the little trees bare to the waist.

They are so far below him! It's as if he were in a plane
and the colonel of his spirit were slowly
waving, waving to whatever it is down there
that thinks he's a god.
Is it the face wet with tears running harder
and harder toward the missed train? Or a
newspaper with big black block letters
blown apart by the wind?

Marsupial, his tools in a pouch,
he might abort them in a long arc out
over the water, over the dull and shimmering
spots of the fish world "where nothing can be burned
and there is no breath."

Will the bridge collapse? Is there a cyst of hope?

Is the sea smaller without fishes?
Will the train be late? Again?
The sea would *be* bigger, but *seem* smaller.
That woman running —
it seems some very important information
is jostling in her purse.

INSTRUMENT OF THE HIGHEST
—Chaim Soutine
(1893–1943)

Ah the truth,

        is the rank lustful lives of men and women

        going after it

in all its *red* —

it is just this nipple exposed beneath the rag

        puce with lava-milk,

it is just this beef-stink in the studio,

the popped-out eyes of rotting salmon,

a particular chicken: the scrawniest one in the shop,

        long neck and blue skin

I'm going to hang it up by the beak with a nail.

In a few days it should be perfect.

It must be *very very* dead.

        Even the red gladioli

have passed over into that garden where things shout

        don't look at me!

Everything startled into still thinking

        it is alive.

What else is spirit but the hectic orifice
                              of the still unwilling
to admit they are excruciatingly gone?

                A conniption fit of fact?

                              Still nothing new.
What is more beautiful than that?

BENT TO EASE US

A century of half-reason
is about to end

A century that knocked every city off its feet
and every family within that city
and every girl and boy within that family
was surprised to discover the century had produced
the richest and happiest people on earth

There was a robin and there was a peach
not to mention a rich population of frogs

There was a machete and there was a murder
ninety-nine million pieces of art and a woman
who never learned how to give birth before
the fetus she carried was left with her arms
in the back of a truck

There was a long line continually forming
of degraded and forsaken bodies marching
toward a blueplate or bluelight special

The light keeps moving
keeps flashing over Angola
over the Azores Aleppo Mullumbimby Sapporo
Calgary and Cannon Beach

It's the global honk of geese made for pâté
while the winter doves in Cartagena
grow fat on white mints

Yes a century of half-reason is about to end
its inconsequential tidbit of glory
franks in the fridge   buns on the shelf

Where were the wings bent to ease us

We all know the way of a god with a girl
mist and hilarity and in a moment
the will is of such an abundance
the small stars at noon can be seen

In no less of a riot
does the light of Venus this very night
feed the seed   the flaggy head
of hard corn-to-be

There were children wearing blindfolds
chasing pigs through the streets

There was a robin and there was a peach
not to mention a rich population of frogs

At this time   after that   then
and it came to pass —
words like gifts
rotting unopened on the beach

APPARITION HILL

There on the scrubby hillside,
among the rocks, she appears
on an evanescent cloud
in a gray gown,
her indescribable face
indescribable.
A shepherdess snuck up the hill for a smoke
and they had a tête-à-tête.
Now the face of the shepherdess
cannot be described.
So it goes. Dot your globes.
Nor can any of the faces
that have looked up at the atomic cloud
be described. Connect the dots.
Fatima, Nagasaki:
that's the beauty of it.
Which the brightest
I asked and lo! he sent a sweet one
to answer me. She stood on a rock
with her dainty feet and explained
it was a finer mistake to suppose
he had sent her, rather than that
which was never intended to be seen.
This caused a mild explosion
in which she floated upwards
while the remnants of her gown
floated down.

CONTINUA

The frozen hills, the silver clouds,
the tracks in the snow leading out of the settlement…
At dusk, the vacant cow making urine.
Should an angel come to Adamant, Vermont
I could not be more shaken.
I would take him by his hand
and walk him up the hill a way,
and show him how the land lies in folds,
like cloth, with all degrees of people digging here and there
for something that suits them, though their shovels
cannot break the roots of poor continua…
and the animals in their bleakhood sheltered by trembling barns,
and those, smaller still, who will be brittle by morning…
and give him, as a parting gift, a child's whistle
from the far north, made in the old way, out of a swan's trachea,
used in summer to call back the birds with great white wings
who have drifted away. Of course no angel comes.
They never do. I keep the whistle, hopelessly broken,
in a box marked *exotic junk*. I lie in bed and pretend
that I have come to understand how we all might be called
back to ourselves and rise, like heated air…
The mousetrap snaps in the middle of the night.
I know what I know what I know
And then I just lie there. Unearthed, but more like a tree
supine, chopped down, its fresh yellow stump
staring upwards.

FAILING TO LIKE HIM

Yesterday you sat in class,
rich and slouching, impressively
dressed to provoke an air of poverty.
Today you nailed a cat upon a cross
and called it Art. Perhaps it was.
I am no expert. I have never read
The Collected Works of Mr. Permissible.
Failing to like him, I am left
a little airless here.
When you were two and first
descended the slide, your joy-shrieks
must have been genuine. Did life
leap up and take you by the neck?
How cognizant you are!
You jerk the cloth off
our secret: we are, some of us, mad.
We wear shower caps. We put milk
in saucers on the floor,
then whiten our teeth.
To show us you are unimpressed
you sport a finger at our smiles.
So this is the scene of our Passion!
I knew an expert once:
hunched over the canvas
with an ultraviolet light
he said *look how the painting
has suffered.*

Each tear had blistered.
The scowling Roman soldier
had lost his young face.

IMPRESARIO

Emma Bovary, after a rendezvous, lifting her skirts
over the fields, though her bottom is drenched with dew —

Lily Bart in the carriage, indignant, hands the man her pearls —

And dear Esther Summerson! holding her ring of housekeeping keys
is beginning to worry while

Fanny Price is beginning to pinken or pale
in want of a cordial for once in her life —

Should I invite them to tea?
Lily wouldn't come.
Emma, in her nervousness, might break a cup
but Esther would mend it —
Fanny in the kitchen would want to be certain:
she ate arsenic *with her hands*?
And then we would serve the tart.

                             I despise muffins.

I despise daisies for that matter
and daffodils are worse.

                             Yellow should not be too bright.

The men understand nothing.

                             They read for humanity's sake.

Or their own intelligence,
whichever is worse.

                             If you give me a brace of pheasants
                             and a case of wine I will tell you

how I like it.

I like to read because
it kills me.

I like it dull.

ECCE HOMO

Wasn't he always muttering to himself,
the surgeon in the sexless hospital
on 99th Street? Twelve steel tables
spanning the length of the lab.
It was an icebox, and each cadaver
wore a white hood like the priests of Easter.
One, unveiled, had mold on his cheek
and his throat was in pieces on the sheet.
We wore beautiful clothes.
Your blue dress. My red shoes.
No sooner had I asked how they died
than I knew no one knew.
You said *I'd like to see a woman*
but the stench around her was so bad
we backed off.
Then the doctor showed us, with a small
shining scalpel, his own procedure
for removing the throat. *It's so simple*
he said *it's beautiful*
and his voice inflated with pride
and that queer drunken grace we carried with us
all the way out to the street
where we stood speechless as brown beer bottles
in snow, speechless as rust on the mailbox
and gray birds, half dead, on their way
to the feeder. How bright the taxis were!
Chrome yellow and coal black.
An elegant man stepped out of one.
The multitudes stopped to stare at him

as if he were Christ
coming to bring home the dead
with his baby talk and a two-day-old beard,
entering the wilderness, inundating it
with our bright and sampled bodies.

EXAMINATION

Out of a high prison window
with a long rope on a dark night John of the Cross
let himself down, a shaking branch
against the moon —

And the Sisters he fled to,
faced with feeding the image of death, fed him
pears stewed with cinnamon! It was enough for him
who lay so long without a spoon to break ardently
into the core.

In the same house there was a Sister
who, like a fussy child coming out of her shadow,
insisted on fresh shoes each time she
approached the altar.

Down five hundred years of vanity
these facts have passed. You must never forget them.
If you tell his story — of how later they brought the pen —

Examine your heart and see if you
leave out the arms of a girl shaking like a branch
as she walks in her new shoes to set down the pears,
two half-moons quivering in their own sweet wine.

DOWN INTO SZECHUAN

We carouse in the evening
tossing down white wine in green jade cups.
No we don't. We hang on the street corners
like dirty monkeys and the dead body next to us
shows its moldy buttocks to the moon.
A foreigner strolls by and takes the snap:
the stinky pimp's limbs have a certain composition
much admired in the West. Living like this
is more difficult than learning to fly. The ancients
are thin and battered in our brains, poetry
is corny, and anyway,
we eat forbidden things — whiskey, Winstons,
plum cunts — at every meal,
while off in the bamboo grove the last of the weirdos
lives, in a kimono with a shaved head.

MID-AUTUMN FESTIVAL

A person to catch fire-flies, and to
try to kindle his household fire with
them. It would be symbolical of something.
                    —among HAWTHORNE'S *notes*

How imaginary! Dull things often are.
It was a dull day Prometheus decided
to fetch some light. Tonight, the Chinese
gaze at the moon by the light of lit goldfish,
paper or plastic. And eating, always symbolic
of something, is de rigueur. Oh dear, another
nut. A plattered pig with electric lights in
his eyes, spiffy and succulent, succinctly there
to remind us of something: Hawthorne's Las Vegas,
the utmost verge of a precipitous absurdity.
And fireworks, wherein we send the stolen goods
back up to heaven. And down they fall.
The gods are quick. Light is gorgeous.
I daresay the candle-snuff, too, leaves
a faint trace of gladness in the air.

DIARY OF ACTION AND REPOSE

In some small sub-station of the universe
the bullfrogs begin to puff out their mouths.
The night-blooming jasmine is fertilized
in the dark. I can smell it.
And then someone unseen and a little ways off
picks up his flute and asserts his identity
in a very sweet way.
I'll throw in the fact it's April in China —
ah exotica, soft night —
while the bullfrog, the jasmine and the flute
form a diary of action that explains my repose:
spring, ripening to her ideal weight, has fallen
from the bough and into my lap.
For twenty minutes the world is perfect
while two or three thinks fumble for their glasses
in my cranium —
ah the impulse to hurt and destroy has arrived
and *oh* into pretty and endless strips it pares the place
round and round —

KINSHIP

Crickets after rain.
Halfway around the world my friend has a martini at four
to celebrate the cessation of weeping.
I don't think of her. I think of the crickets,
a devalued equivalent, but they are light as matchsticks
and can mate on a leaf. Imagine that. We are gigantic
and mating on anything less than a chair is hard to imagine.
Our tears are small, dew really, though they can and often do
run together and then they must be just about the size of rain
that batters the streets and leaves and the roofs of cars.
Come to think of it, the cessation of weeping is mighty
and the crickets are good to sing to it, afterwards,
though it is still dark, and long before we think of loving.

QUITE PERSONAL

Frankly, a funeral can be quite personal, but
it's so sporty now to tote your video onto
the grass and point it at what will last and
last: will the video be quite personal then?
What's preferable to the corpse's brother
quoting anecdotes? Something quite solemn?
Say the video is solemn then
and when the mourners gather together
to watch it, they'll eat meat loaf
and the video being so solemn and so sad
will make the meat loaf quite personal,
for something warm and on our lap can do that
sometimes, when we least expect it.
On the other hand, if the video is too personal
the meat loaf will seem cold and impersonal
and no one will pay it the slightest bit
of attention. In this way everything eludes me.

TOWARDS THE CORRECTION
OF YOUTHFUL IGNORANCE

There was a carriage in the story and when it rumbled
over the cobblestones one caught a glimpse
of the gas-lit face inside....

But the young men, after reading "The Dead"
by James Joyce, sauntered out of the classroom
and agreed: "it's *puerile*, that's what it is."

Are there no more mothers who lay yellowing
in their gowns? Am I to insist, when I hate my desk,
my galoshed legs shoved in under, and all
Christmas dinners right down to eternity — ?

When I was younger I wandered out to the highway
and saw a car with its windshield beautifully cracked.
The blood on the seat was so congealed
and there was so much of it, I described it to no one.

When I was younger I did not think
I would live to see the cremation of my youth,
then the hair on my arms went up in flames
along with my love for Nelson Giles.

Now I saunter out in the lamb-like snow
where the black squirrels leap from bough
to bough, gobbling everything.

The snowflakes are pretty in a way.
The young men know that and compact them into balls.
When they hit my windshield I begin to laugh.

I think they are right after all:
there's no love in this world

but it's a beautiful place.
Let their daughters keep the diaries,
careful descriptions of boys in the dark.

FUNNY STORY

I don't remember where I was going.
I always worry about driving in the snow.
To the airport I think.
What if my car won't start, cold as it is?
But at five a.m. on the morning of January fifth
I was up and out.
Quite frankly, I can still see it:
the sky a glaze of celadon
with a pink moon set in the corner.
It took my breath away
in small white puffs.
When I get to thinking, I think maybe it was my mood.
But my mood was low-down and mean.
I mean before I saw it.
Afterwards — no, not afterwards:
in the same moment
I realized I have a prerequisite for joy.
It surprised me.
I was surprised to consider everything must be made of glass.
Not only the icy poverty of life on earth
but high, immovable things.
I was afraid to move.
I was afraid I would be late.
I was afraid my car wouldn't start.
What if the moon, awash as it was
in decanted light, was dangerously close
to disappearing altogether
and for good this time?
So I just stood there.

I let it take my breath away.
That's OK I said
take my breath away.
And it was gone.

ALWAYS IN A MANGER

Spring, season of Bartleby,
some prefer not to be green:

the suicide dangling in a barn
crowded with hay while the cat
in the corner licks the last of the sacs
off her litter:

I cut the rope off his neck
and saw to it the new ones
were bagged and dropped in
a pond.

Lord strengthen the view:

the clouds sparring, unleavened
grasses and new-whited hillocks.

The ruff grouse drumming
drove the man mad.
On more than one occasion he warned me
those wings were in his chest
hot with sheer life.

I guess he got his senses mixed.
Spring's a sorrow to us all.

Sap and wind. Whenever he walked into
the barn he said in a breath
Christ, I'm always in a manger.

Then the afterthought
flies will be born in the sockets of my eyes.

And then I remembered some words
my wife had over her Christmas card:
Peace & Joy

Just how do you figure
they get along?

WHITE TULIPS

Surprised girl of the north!
Someone's desiderata, not mine:
she was sweet and boozey
and deranged my bowels.

Blanched
as a country wedding,
the soused bride
and her black-eyed groom.

Mosquitoless,
thank heaven.
In a pasture of duds
the negligee spirit with a portwine stain
develops a passion to be the pointing-stock
of every finger,
every upright white there is.

FOUNTAINHEAD OF
ESOTERIC KNOWLEDGE

I stand idly, magnanimous and sinister,
fingering the inventory, the adorable ghosts
of little shelf lives that are gone or half-
used up, while the poison pools in my blood
and the mercury lurks in the thermometer:
aspirin, daughter of the willow sap, fidelity
in a pellet; dentifrice, son of the gleaming Swede
who fell in battle and has lain there whitening
ever since; and a grape elixir saved only by codeine,
warlord of the drowsy. Vitamins, the too many
children of the alphabet, and small batons,
a cotton stop on each end, for marching into the ear.
Saline, vial of tears (expires 9/90) and Hypotears
Pluto and Persephone shed. A rolled veil of gauze
tissued in a box for the lunatic bride or her invalid
sister. Squit-pot of Formula 500 with squalene,
a deep secret deposited only in shark livers,
preferably off the coast of Japan. Nail lacquer
in *oyster.* Floss (for restringing pearls) and
astringent, a noose for the pores. Mint Julep Mask,
mostly kaolin, a fine white clay named after a hill
in China, adulterated here to a green clownish Ming
marketed to remind one of New Orleans. Bee pollen,
golden viscous globs to induce wandering and return.
Crushed Rose, Hibiscus, Ginger Jam, slick sticks
who swivel up and eat my lips, and their friends,
a shadow box of horrors in *beechen green, taupe vert,*
silversmoke fawn. Cheek cream to induce the astonishment

poets are famous for, a wand of mascara and a linear
starfish, sandpapered on both sides. My gooseflesh
rises: razor blades in their steel book might
explain the plot, but their pages are disposable,
and destined for the keyless chink.

ZORRO & THE BATS

Leaf-chinned, fringe-lipped, hammer-headed, tube-
nosed, disk-winged, funnel-eared and sucker-footed
      they fly — and I know for a fact God
despises them. Eight million years ago they were
      black handkerchiefs waving in total despair
at the lack of belfries: a satanical fetus
      in search of a church in a crepuscular
swoop. Then one day while they were sleeping
      the swallows stole their flight pattern, adding
Lamborghini wings and a much-needed mask.
      By 1983 they would serve the United States
Navy as living proof radar on any scale is not
      what it's cracked up to be. But by then
there would be an endangered species extinguished
      every hour. We did not see it coming. We
may now set our watches, and make a Zorro-like
      X at every little leap of the hand.
O my darkling chevrons! You know we could care less
      and are glad, almost happy, in your sonic speech
over our heads where the attic vaults, an inverted ark
      you've built for yourselves in the dark.

RETURNING FROM THE OPERA
I SPY A WOOD DUCK

You! A living tonic in your shocking cap,
unseen, unknown, who persists in the shade,
is there, undreamt, molded and tufted
in a feral spree of unspoken freshness:
the acid drake! A streak of green, the violet
fluff — though death be bleach
the sight of you will dwell in hell with me
when I go there, outburn, outbright
the brittle and little bodies of my kind
who pitted themselves with painted light.
Who by his own cant can see your beam
and not know you are dear to a malevolent heart?
Floating two-eyed temple
you have in you, when you preen,
what knocks me senseless on the floor:
a living priest in flames
singing o-ignite-me-more!

CHINOISERIE

I've been up half the night
reading bad translations of Chinese poetry
which I delight in as I delight
in failures of the sublime kind

like the shoe thrown clear across the room
to where it lands in a delirious heap, its tongue
open, eyes abashed, laces in the lax curlicues
of a curious decline.

I've been up half the night
as though I were young and could personally
nudge the dawn.
O those Tang grand-dads!

The flying cranes of their time!
I grow wild without sleep and throw myself
at their prime. My cries wake an old man
who has fallen asleep in a boat

on the Yellow River and save him
from being swept away. But since I have disturbed
his dream, he is stand-offish and does not
offer me his mellowing wine.

BUTTERNUT GUTTER

The first solitary bird of morning hitting its notes
against the night, *what does it know*
as I fumble in the first sweet failings of dark
for the clock with its luminous rays?

A portion of my life has been drowned.
I have bled to death in my dreams, I have flown,
I have ridden a white horse through snow so deep
only its head and my hands could be seen,
and I have even, in my dreams,
seen the sunset fold up
like a lacquered fan.

But never this. Never the piercing or dusky
strut of a day's first inch.
To be truthful, nine times out of ten
I wake to the wilderness of Butternut Gutter
without my glasses, and the unfocused earth
welcomes me back as the prodigal daughter
of her dreams. But I can't be wakened.
Oh, one day I may wake and want
a crate of champagne, shouting
*Appearance? Reality? One man's desert
is my spiritual icechest.*

But not today. And the bird?
It sits, evangelized by the light,
in a niche covered with ivy.
Another marvel of the earth

I have tried to escape, always
to escape, as a bird does
out of a cage. Is that unnatural?
Is that a great crime?

HOW IT IS

Things begin to burgeon. The peas go gallivanting
in their pods. That old spring prop, birdsong, wafts
through the trees, the trees with their leaves lit
like the underside of the sea. We walk deep inside
and have a picnic there. In the filtered gloss of
the forest, pears come out of our pockets and
lunch proceeds. All this is pleasant and I will
erase it. I will erase it because the height of insanity
demands that I do. The height of insanity says we were
in a field under a festoon of clouds. The height of insanity
says I was not there. The height of insanity says
I have not had a happy life. The height of insanity
says it was snowing, insists that I say *in the heaven
of February, in a porcelain snow.* I will erase it.
The heaven of February knows I was there, in the woods
on the twenty-second of April, eating. My hand goes
to my mouth. There is horror in my eyes. How do I know?
The martinet in a boiled shirt says it is so.
Christ, I've had a happy life! But who am I to know?

ANCIENT CUSTOM

I saw the farfetched rose erect on the bush, slightly
unfurled, its curious stare both blank
and beckoning. My glance set off its innermost
secret, a scented silence I smelled at once.
I *had* to touch it, I was almost afraid to
but I did, as I would a fevered brow
about to die. Unable to bear it any longer
I made my mouth small like a bee
and came down on the rose, over all of its petals
until the whole rose was in my mouth and blossomed
not in this world but in me. I drank its dew.
I lifted my head and knew water was dry.
I wanted other roses. After others, more.
I could not rest until the whole garden
had been guessed at and was mine.
Rose after rose after rose
The blank stares! The red nights!

CABBAGES

The blues and greens, the reds,
the purples, the blanched pearls.
The smocked farmer delivers two heads
at the same time, pulling them up
like a pair of balanced pails.
The children wail. The quartered brainchild
lies upon their plates. Cut, they are swirly-
full of fancy French end papers and strange
lacunas. A bumper crop is in the air:
China stinks of cabbage soaked in brine,
wet and rotten. They feed a billion
on the cannonballs. They pile them in
the streets, they build a wall, they
roll heads until the feathers shed. In
Ireland there's a lidded pot and they're
blindfolded. Their mouths are stuffed in
Poland. They're doll-sized in Flanders,
to be discreet. Such a loss
of mind! It's fodder for the imagination.
While we live & shout & die, they are
capable of escaping the least of attention
and so survive: thrown into a river
they float, crowding helplessly towards
an alien sea.

HAINAN ISLAND

I stand at the tropical edge
where the little waves go *swoosh*
and there are no bathers turning over
like strips of bacon.
There are thirty-six thousand days
in a life. I've come a long way
to see such beauty.
And it *is* beautiful. There are egg-like
rocks where I sit and drink my wine.
I can't help but think of home:
the cold stone steps outside
my door, from where I watch
the tower of a dead tree
untossed by the wind.

MEMOIR

Five days rain and I see waterless Charles
reduced to brandishing his brain & pistol:
flashback of rain & rain on the stony fields
of Flores, that blind & blue island gone to
honey, hydrangea mostly, sealed in glass with
cork & wax. The colored label showed a cloudless

sky. Lie. No mailboats November-May. Six months
letterless, I read Doughty, who made a study of
the Bedouin retina, who made me weep, so unflinchingly
sweet was he, longing to get through and go on,
take care of his camel and speak Good English
in spite of the sun. He was also willing to Perish

but lived to bathe before dining with the Consul.
Was it Planned or Unplanned? That was his exam.
The old book smelled of moths & gloves. Continuous
rain glazes my garden. It spices the air.
Flores must be misted in and the driest desert
dead: moot points. Placebos of madness. Test me.

ARTURO'S SONG

No sparkles in the brain-pan.
I shall be a dazing one
all of my days.

After the olives ripen in Tuscany
there is no second sorrow.

When I am sad I have nothing to say
and when I am happy speak freely
of my sorrow.

DOVE

I

One thousand years ago a woman in Japan
with no name
wrote a book without a title.
I can turn the pages
I can rip them out
and fold them,
put them in my pocket
and walk into town. She said
even at the best of times
I am not much good at poetry
and at a moment like this
I feel quite incapable of expressing myself.
But one day the pages will blacken and curl
like singed eyelashes. And that will be
that. So why walk to town?

2

My heart is full of malice
and it will not burn away.
Of course there was Yeats, *stony*
in front of the fire, but he was
himself and I am mine, I like
to stand in the street
with a large tear
caught in my lashes, like the petit-

bourgeois I am.
I do say this is so
I do say I have seen a black wing
I stood in the street
when the dove of her soul
broke out of the book
and flew from the burning earth.

TOM PAINE'S GRAVE

Fourscore and seven years ago Lincoln spoke
spoke my father in 1950. He had come to see
the battlefield and having no memory
of either occasion I am inclined to memorize
the President's speech and my father's words
and having no children it is doubtful I will
repeat the words in two more score years, which
would not be true anyway and the children would
not be young. Years pass like the turtledoves
who eat and shit in the same breath, but the
untrue and unyoung remain. *All is mystery and
hazard* Tom Paine wrote in Paris, a great city,
where today the peoples are met to speak of
Antarctica, testing whether that nation so conceived
and so dedicated can long endure. They have
come to dedicate a portion of that field as
a final resting place for wildlife. It is
altogether fitting and proper that they should
do this, for it is within their power to add or
detract. But in a larger sense they cannot consecrate
anything. We little note nor long remember everything
that is said, in light of the unfinished work of
the years, which pass, and the unyoung and untrue
which remain. No one knows where Tom Paine's grave
is, or I would go there alone and in silence and
place Lincoln's top hat on the spot,
like a penguin, petulant on his rim of ice.

TRUST ME

What can be discussed in words
I beg to state in brief.
A man has only one death:
it may be as light as goose down
or as heavy as a fatted hog.
Gingerly, the flowers open
and are crushed in the vat.
What's in your new perfume?
The hills of Africa are in it,
and the cormorants with their mouths full of fish,
a bed of carnations, a swannery in Switzerland,
the citrine sun baking Nappa
and a rhino whining at the moon.
An after-dinner argument is in it
and the every-stronger doses of clap-trap
we are forced to take while still alive.
A whole aeroplane, wings and all,
and the lush spaghetti siphoned into lips
poised for a kiss.
Finish it, finish it.

A FEW WORDS TO LET IN DOUBT

Surely my mother is putting gold leaf on God's
cake tonight, for on earth she was enamored of
the *charlotte russe*, searching the art shops
for an edible gilt. When she lit the five candles
on the buttercream skirt of a centered doll whose
flaxen hair burst into flames, blow as I might,
I could not save the day. This afternoon I use
a paint scraper, my forefinger and thumb, to pull
ribbons of white chocolate for the bridal torte;
like so. The passion for adornment is finally toil.
A contented and floury pastry chef points out to me
Mr. Keats precedes his famous poem on fame
with the added touch of a proverb: you cannot
eat your cake and have it too. *It is as if*
the rose should pluck herself Or the ripe plum
finger its misty bloom. So I tuck white violets
into the crevice between tiers and shrug.
They have the faintest purple centers
like a small hidden heart
and the knife is solid silver
with a long ribboned handle.

OUT OF THE GARDEN

How I long to leave the party
its wicker and cucumber
leave my long-stemmed glass on the table
walk out of the garden   meet you at the Moon Wink Motel
and show you my garters   my stinking breath
the havoc it makes in close quarters
The clouds lash themselves into foam
The bush is drooling with currants
All of my guests turn to see the moon-sized sun
sink in its fashionable blood
The ochre of pollen smears as it falls
from the lily   I want the world abstract
general   vague   I want the world without
details   wickerless   cucumberless
So lumbering and insane does the showing seem
So precise seems the telling
the impossible telling which is impossible
to say   while the corn is high   so high
While it is high let me put down
my lavender cocktail
and say I loathe the exact

ONCE AND FOR ALL

I

Let me complain of your love.
I am not your Tartar girl.
My eyes do not flash, nor do I
rise and dance. Nevertheless
it's a singsong world. I see
the orioles. I see your scrotum.
I see the verdigris domes
of European capitols rising like
cabbages. And if my legs have lately
been on your back, they make the sound
of the word *husked*, both naked and
clothed. If I have a seed
it will germinate in the ground
and grow wheat.
And the Tartar girls will drive
the tractors, and feed the world.

II

Love, let me apologize.
The old pair sit on either side
of the bread. He picks up the knife.
The knife picks up the light and
the light picks up her eyes.
She nods. He cuts. It is difficult
to perform. There are prayers

that are not even touching,
but they wring out my mouth
when they rise.

UNBELIEVABLE

There's the moon hung by a thread again.
Unbelievable. I'm in my own little world.
Are you in yours?

Empress Lu did this to Lady Ch'i:
cut off her hands, cut off her feet,
put out her eyes.

She could lie on her back like the new laid moon.
It still happens today, along the borders
of Burma and in American neighborhoods.

The thread of humanity is long and strong.
I have hands and I have feet.
I can walk to your house and have a look.

But if I lived there, I would do things
differently. Sometimes in my sleep I roll
and grunt. Empress Lu called Lady Ch'i

her *little human pig.* "She is *divine!*"
the empress squealed. Once I saw a man on the
pedestrian steps: legless, he used his hands

to hoist himself up from step to step, stopping
to breathe. There were one hundred steps
or more. Not to mention the moon.

THE QUEEN OF CONSTRICTION

"I am as lonely as . . . as Franz Kafka."
—FRANZ KAFKA

Leafy outside the window. A little bird with
a mermaidish figure flies down to the rain-polished
branch and shakes. A man brings me something to eat
without disturbing me. It is a dream scene. On
Thursdays I mop. I swing the thing. Black water
results. A vile thing with far too many legs
must be escorted out. I too am removable,
especially the head parts. But who would know?
All those lashy legs chachacha across the spatula.
I might as well be in China. Where I am.
With concrete here and concrete there, here
a block, there a block, everywhere a block
block. I look at Miss Legs: poesy in the year
2000 will have offspring like this. Oh my!
I'll chuck it off the balcony all the same:
which is what I do now and watch her fall
seven stories to the court below
where she lands without a shake and goes
on her many ways. Crackers cum laude for lunch.
Why I never shall marry is plain:
an act of constriction is needed
during these long and dumbfounded days.

TIMBERLAND

Paul's Fish Fry in Bennington, Vermont, is no longer
Closed For The Season Reason Freezin. The umbrellas
have opened over the picnic tables and the bees are
beginning to annoy the french fries, the thick shakes
and real malts of my past:

I am thirteen thousand miles removed, on the delta
of the Pearl River, eating a litchi. Its translucent flesh just
burst in my mouth; shreds of it glitter between my teeth.
I smile but the fruit seller is sour. In fact, he is so sour
the only man on earth he resembles is Paul. But the litchi...

Actually none of this has happened yet. I am nineteen
years old. I am riding in the boxcar of a freight train
hurtling towards Pocatello, Idaho. In a very dangerous move
I maneuver my way back to the car behind me, an open gondola
carrying two tons of timberland eastward out of Oregon:

it is here I will lie all night, my head against the logs,
watching the stars. No one knows where I am. My mother thinks
I am asleep in my bed. My friends, having heard of a derailment
at ninety miles an hour on the eastbound freight, think I am
dead. But I'm here, hurtling across the continent with un-

believable speed. We are red hot and we go, the steel track
with its imperceptible bounce allows us to go, our circuitous
silhouette against the great Blue Mountains and my head in a
thrill watching the stars: I am not yet at a point in my life
where I am able to name them, but there are so many and they are

so white! I'm hurtling toward work at Paul's, toward the litchi-bite in Guangzhou, toward the day of my death alright, but all I can say is I am *happyhappyhappy* to be here with the stars and the logs, with my head thrown back and then pitched forward in tears. And the litchi! it's like swallowing a pearl.

XINGANG ZHONG LU

The pig's lungs,
meshy sacs of fat and mother-of-pearl
repose nicely on the butcher block,
edible bagpipes.
You may not understand how people
can eat such things.
But let me tell you, there are those
who, in the same manner, cannot
eat poetry.
Do you scoff at tourists?
Poetry is a tourist.
It wears several cameras
around its neck
and takes nice pictures
of deadly things.
It cannot be impoverished
and that is its prize.
How welcome the busloads
after the war!
I live on Xingang Zhong Lu
and I am a tourist.
Were I not here, the butcher
would be inexplicably sad.
I give him more money for his lungs
than his lungs are worth.

IDYLL

I was trotting to market with my basket for greens
       when a wandering nude seemed to spring from the ground:
he took me down a peg or two, that pantless man made matte
       with grime, who hid his penis with one hand and smoked
with the other; pocketless, I presume penniless, he must have
       leaned and picked his stub from the trash-hill heaped
on every corner. I said *pantless*, like the billionaire lord
       in his penthouse tower looking down on his mistress.
We passed. I'm tall. His cock was huge. His hands were small.
       The stalls were going up around us in an aimless
no-place-to-put-it style and the great white ginger blooming
       in a lake of galvanized buckets when he blushed
with the blood of an ox: I fell all the way down the pegs then,
       thinking ah! we are both ashamed, when all
the dirty vegetables glowed, they glowed in a grisly way,
       yellow and ochre and orange, kooky and blunderous
as his cock: the calloused white radishes, the tender chives
       deprived of sunlight, even the crawling flies, the hanging
sides of beef, the blackened fowl on a spit and the snakes coiled
       in water, for sale, silver for the eating. He sat on
the ground and his penis was nothing really, just the sad detail
       of a terrible event: when he touched it a pigeon
perked up. In a fertile field at sunset did he throw water
       on the crop? Did he lift the wooden ladle, his back
bending and rising so the water went spuming in an arc of light?
       Did he leave his village at night? Was there a moon?
Did he desire a job, an oafish sum of cash? For he's drifting
       among millions now, as nondescript as Adam, the same guy
who once stood single in the floral field then presto! disappeared.

PERFECT EXAMPLE

O my friend, your imponderabilia
frightens me. The moon is beclouded
and still she whitens the night.
You must believe me when I tell you
it makes no difference that
Armstrong walked on its chalk.
You must not drink too much
or you will forget her gleam
is upon us. It is as though
a severed head rolled in
and stopped at your feet. I know
life goes on; I know lunch ferments
in your stomach and you burp.
But in the seventh century
a space began to appear between
each word of a text. How the space
opens between the moon and her cloud!
My heart twists into the Celtic knot
of a hamhock. Once more,
my mind's eloped. I know what
you're thinking: poetry, a sphinx
in a sandstorm. What did you eat
for lunch? Small green onions,
kippers and lemon curd? You have
a head as big as a white mule's
and nothing in it.

ENTIRELY, EVENTUALLY

The afternoon digresses into evening,
autumn into snow.
Tu Fu and Li Po met, and then they parted,
and who's to say which day was their digression?
Such poems of departure are not possible today:
we sail forward and fly back like a loving pair
of purple mandarin ducks.
Who leaves for the mountains and never comes back?
No one I know. I turned on the television
and there was a man on channel two
talking about perfume.
A man on channel three was lost in the mountains
and his dog kept smelling things.
After that I went over to the window
and was surprised to see it was light.
I thought of sleep, a major digression.
But I couldn't sleep. I kept thinking
about that man on the mountain.
After he made that movie I'm sure
he went home and made love to his wife.
And then maybe he ate some eggs.
But it breaks my heart to think
he is bound to lose the thread entirely,
eventually.